C.L.HANON   T.BAKER

HANON

THE VIRTUOSO PIANIST

IN SIXTY EXERCISES

FOR THE PIANO

BOOK III

Copyright © 2018 Millennium Multimedia
International Copyright Secured All Rights Reserved

Table of Contents

Preface	iii
C.L. Hanon – Exercise N°44	6
C.L. Hanon – Exercise N°45	8
C.L. Hanon – Exercise N°46	11
C.L. Hanon – Exercise N°47	15
C.L. Hanon – Exercise N°48	17
C.L. Hanon – Exercise N°49	20
C.L. Hanon – Exercise N°50	21
C.L. Hanon – Exercise N°51	24
C.L. Hanon – Exercise N°52	27
C.L. Hanon – Exercise N°53	32
C.L. Hanon – Exercise N°54	37
C.L. Hanon – Exercise N°55	39
C.L. Hanon – Exercise N°56	41
C.L. Hanon – Exercise N°57	49
C.L. Hanon – Exercise N°58	55
C.L. Hanon – Exercise N°59	57
C.L. Hanon – Exercise N°60	59

PREFACE

The study of the piano is now-a-days so general, and good pianists are so numerous, that mediocrity on this instrument is no longer endured. In consequence, one must study the piano eight or ten years before venturing to perform a piece of any difficulty, even at a gathering of amateurs. Now, how few persons are in a position to devote so many years to this study! It often happens, therefore, that for want of sufficient practice the playing is uneven and incorrect. The left hand gives out in passages of slight difficulty; the fourth and fifth fingers are almost useless for lack of special exercises for these fingers, which are always weaker than the rest; and when passages in octaves, in tremolo or trills occur, they are usually executed only by dint of exertion and fatigue, so that the performance is very incorrect and wholly wanting in expression.

For several years we have labored to overcome this state of affairs, making it our aim to unite in one work special exercises which render possible a complete course of pianistic study in far less time.

To attain this end, it sufficed to find the solution of the following problem :
If all five fingers of the hand were absolutely equally well trained, they would be ready to execute anything written for the instrument, and the only question remaining would be that of fingering, which could be readily solved.

We have found the solution of this problem in our work "The Virtuoso-Pianist, in 60 Exercises," etc. In this volume will be found the exercises necessary for the acquirement of agility, independence, strength and perfect evenness in the fingers, as well as suppleness of the wrists – all indispensable qualities for fine execution; furthermore, these exercises are calculated to render the left hand equally skilful with the right. Excepting a few exercises, to be found in several methods, the entire book is our personal work. These exercises are interesting, and do not fatigue the student like the generality of five-finger exercises, which are so dry that one requires the perseverance of a true artist to summon up courage to study them.

These exercises are written in such a manner that, after having read them a few times, they can be played in quite a rapid movement; they thus become excellent practice for the fingers, and one loses no time in studying them. If desired, any of these exercises may be played on several pianos simultaneously, rousing a spirit of emulation among the students, and habituating them to ensemble-playing.

All descriptions of difficulties will be met with. The exercises are so arranged, that in each successive number the fingers are rested from the fatigue caused by the one preceding. The result of this combination is, that all mechanical difficulties are executed without effort or weariness; and, after such practice, the fingers attain to astonishing facility of execution.

This work is intended for all piano-pupils. It may be taken up after the pupil has studied about a year. As for more advanced students, they will study it in a very short time, and will thereafter never experience the stiffness which may have been previously felt in fingers or wrists; this will render them capable of surmonting the principal mechanical difficulties.

Pianists and teachers who cannot find time for sufficient practice to keep up their playing, need only to play these exercises a few hours in order to regain all the dexterity of their fingers.

This entire volume can be played through in an hour; and if, after it has been thoroughly mastered, it be repeated daily for a time, difficulties will disappear as if by enchantment, and that beautiful, clear, clean, pearling execution will have been acquired which is the secret of distinguished artists.

Finally, we offer this work as giving the key to all mechanical difficulties. We therefore consider that we are rendering a real service to young pianists, to teachers, and to the directors of boarding-schools, in proposing their adoption of our work, "The Virtuoso Pianist."

Charles-Louis Hanon
translated by Dr. Theodore Baker

THE VIRTUOSO PIANIST

PART III

Exercises 44-60

Virtuoso Exercises, for Obtaining a Mastery over the Greatest Mechanical Difficulties.

Notes repeated in groups of three.

Lift the fingers high and with precision, without raising hand or wrist. As soon as the first four measures are well learned, take up the rest of the exercise.

C.L. HANON

Notes repeated in groups of two, by all five fingers.

Study the first fingering until it is thoroughly mastered; practise similarly each of the five following fingerings then play through the whole exercise without stopping.

3rd fingering.

4th fingering.

The Trill for all five fingers.

Practise the first 6 measures until they can be executed in quite a rapid tempo; then practise the rest of the trill. Where the fingering is changed (1), be careful that not the slightest unevenness is apparent.

It is of interest to note that Mozart used this exercise for the study of the trill.

Thalberg's trill.

Notes repeated in groups of four.

Lift the fingers high and with precision throughout this exercise, without raising hand or wrist. When the first line is mastered, and not before, take up the rest of the exercise.

Wrist-exercise.

Detached Thirds and Sixths.

Lift the wrists well after each stroke, holding the arms perfectly quiet; the wrist should be supple, and the fingers firm without stiffness. Practise the first four measures until an easy wrist-movement is obtained; then take up the rest of the exercise.

Detached Sixths.

Same remarks as for the thirds.

Stretches from the 1st to the 4th fingers, and from the 2nd to the 5th, in each hand.

Very useful for increasing the stretching-capacity of these fingers.

(M.M. ♩ = 60 to 108)

Continuation of the preceding exercise.

(M.M. ♩ = 60 to 108)

Legato Thirds.

We recommend careful study of this exercise, as Thirds occupy a very important place in difficult music. All notes must be struck evenly and very distinctly.

(M.M. ♩ = 40 to 84)

50.

Scales in Legato Thirds.

It is indispensable to practise scales in legato thirds. To obtain a smooth legato, keep the fifth finger of the right hand for an instant on its note while the thumb and 3rd finger are passing over to the next third; in the left hand, the thumb is similarly held for an instant. Notes to be held are indicated by half-notes. (1) Proceed similarly in the chromatic scale further on, and in all scales in Thirds.

Chromatic scales in minor thirds.

Preparatory Exercise for Scales in Octaves.

The wrists should be very supple, the fingers taking the octaves should be held firmly but without stiffness, and the unoccupied fingers should assume a slightly rounded position.

At first repeat these three first lines slowly until a good wrist-movement is attained, and then accelerate the tempo, continuing the exercise without interruption. If the wrists become fatigued, play more slowly until the feeling of fatigue has disappeared, and then gradually accelerate up to the first tempo.

See remarks to № 48.

Scales in Thirds, in the Keys Most Used.

Play these scales legato, and very evenly; it is highly important to master them thoroughly. *See remarks to № 50.*

Scales in Octaves in the 24 Keys.

First practise each of these scales until it can be executed with facility; then play through all 24 without interruption.

We cannot too strongly insist on the absolute necessity of a proper wrist-movement; it is the only means of executing octaves without stiffness, and with suppleness vivacity and energy.

See the explanations for № 48 and 51.

(1) In all scales in Octaves, the black keys are to be taken with the 4th finger of either hand.

The Fourfold Trill in Thirds, for all five fingers.

Execute this exercise very smoothly and evenly, striking each Third very clearly.

The Threefold Trill.

Same remark as for № 54.

Special fingerings for the fourfold Trill.

another fingering

Scales in Broken Octaves, in the 24 Keys.

Play them through without stopping.
This highly important exercise likewise prepares the wrists for the study of the tremolo.

(1) Throughout this exercise, take the black keys with the 4th finger of each hand.

Broken Arpeggios in Octaves, in the 24 Keys.

To begin with, practise the first arpeggio in C, which must be played cleanly and distinctly, with a good wrist-movement, before passing to the next in minor.

Similarly practise each of the 24 arpeggios; then play them all through without interruption.

(1) Throughout this exercise, take the black keys with the 4th finger of each hand.

(1) As this arpeggio, and the next one in Eb minor, are on black keys alone, it makes no difference whether the 4th or the 5th finger be employed.

Sustained Octaves.

Strike the octaves vigorously without lifting the wrists, nd hold them down while deftly executing the intermediate notes with a good finger-movement.

Fourfold Trill in Sixths, for the combination of the 1st and 4th, and 2nd and 5th fingers of each hand.

Neither hand nor wrist should be moved in the least while playing this exercise.

(M.M. ♩ = 40 to 84)

The Tremolo.

To properly execute the tremolo, it should be played with the same rapidity as the roll on the drum.

Practise slowly at first, then gradually accelerate the tempo until the movement indicated (M.M. ♩ = 72) is reached. Finally, by oscillations of the wrists, the rapidity is still further augmented up to the tempo of the drum-roll. This etude is long and difficult; but the excellent result will fully repay the pianist for the trouble and fatigue encountered. Steibelt made his hearers shiver by his execution of the tremolo.

Concluding Remarks.

Now that the student has practised this entire volume, he is acquainted with the chief mechanical difficulties; but, if he would enjoy the fruit of his toil, and become a real virtuoso, he ought to play this entire book through every day for a certain time; only in this way can he familiarize himself with these great difficulties. An hour is required to play the book through.

The greatest artists find it necessary to repeat daily exercises for several hours, merely to "keep up their playing." We should not, therefore be accused of exaggerating the matter when we require of a student aspiring to true virtuosity, that he should play these exercises through every day.

Printed in Great Britain
by Amazon